Start Sailing

Andy Smith & Tim

fernhurst
BOOKS

Copyright © Fernhurst Books 1999

First published in 1999 by
Fernhurst Books
Duke's Path, High Street,
Arundel, West Sussex, BN18 9AJ
Tel 01903 882277
Fax 01903 882715
email sales@fernhurstbooks.co.uk
web www.fernhurstbooks.co.uk

Write, phone or fax us for a free,
full colour brochure.

British Library Cataloguing in Publication Data:
A catalogue record for this book is available from
the British Library

ISBN 1 898660 55 7

Drawings by Ann Winterbotham

Cover design by Simon Balley

Cover photo by Ocean Images

Designed by Creative Byte

Printed in China through World Print

The authors and publisher would like to thank
James Stevens of the RYA for the original concept
and Rockley Watersports for their week's hospitality
and loan of boats. The photo on page 1 is by Ocean
Images and on page 33 courtesy of The Laser Centre.
The boat template is based on plans kindly donated
by the Wayfarer Association.

Contents

Foreword

Sailing a dinghy on a breezy day is one of the most exhilarating outdoor activities, but it takes skill and practice.

The best way to learn is to follow an ordered and well-tested training scheme taught by an RYA coach. On his courses and in this book Andy Smith breaks the subject into easily understandable sections so the beginner can grasp the basics and start sailing competently and safely. The order follows the 'RYA Method' and is used by hundreds of sailing schools throughout Europe.

Andy has taught all levels of sailing from beginner to instructor over twenty years. He is one of the RYA's most experienced Coaches and uses here the same clear straightforward style as he does on the water. If you follow the advice in this book or, even better, use it as background reading on a course you should be in control of a sailing dinghy in a few days.

Good sailing!

James Stevens
National Coach

Flow diagram for teaching method

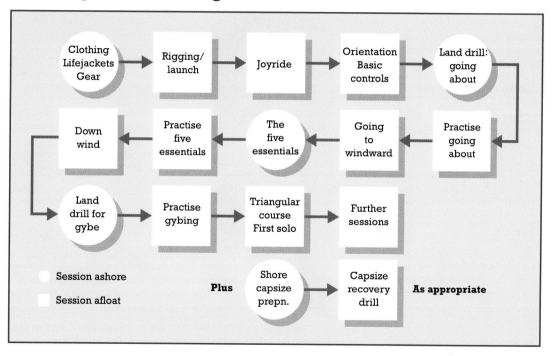

Safety

Common sense is the best adviser. Know your limitations: are you and your crew fit enough? Are you properly dressed?

Clothing

In order of increasing expense, you can wear:

Waterproofs.

A wetsuit (usually a long john, with a bolero top). Water can get in, but is loosely trapped and warms up.

A steamer (like a wetsuit, but has seals at the neck, wrists and feet).

A dry top (waterproof, with seals at neck, wrists and waist).

A dry suit.

Fifty per cent of heat loss is through the head, so a hat is essential in cold weather.

Good footwear stops you stubbing your toes and grips in the wet.

A buoyancy aid is less bulky, but simply helps you stay afloat. Look for the EN393 label.

A lifejacket (left) is bulky, but will keep you afloat with your face out of the water, even when you're unconscious. Look for the EN 395 label. On a lifejacket look to see how many Newtons/Kilograms of buoyancy it provides, and match up to your weight.

Parts of the boat

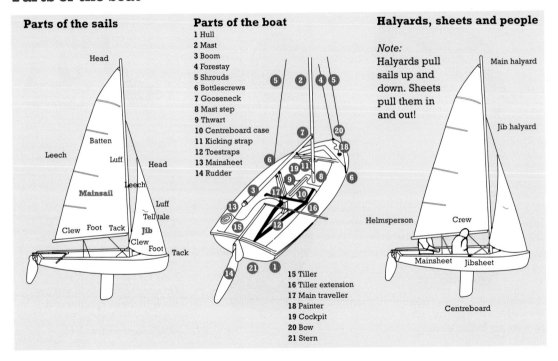

Parts of the sails

Head

Leech

Batten

Luff

Mainsail

Leech

Luff

Clew Foot Tack

Head

Tell tale

Jib

Clew Foot

Tack

Parts of the boat

1 Hull
2 Mast
3 Boom
4 Forestay
5 Shrouds
6 Bottlescrews
7 Gooseneck
8 Mast step
9 Thwart
10 Centreboard case
11 Kicking strap
12 Toestraps
13 Mainsheet
14 Rudder

15 Tiller
16 Tiller extension
17 Main traveller
18 Painter
19 Cockpit
20 Bow
21 Stern

Halyards, sheets and people

Note:
Halyards pull sails up and down. Sheets pull them in and out!

Main halyard

Jib halyard

Helmsperson   Crew

Mainsheet   Jibsheet

Centreboard

Rigging

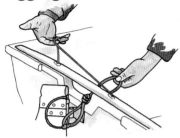

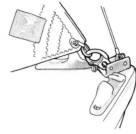

1 Put on the rudder. Lead the downhaul rope under the traveller.

2 Find the sailmakers' mark on the jib, and fix this corner to the bow.

3 Run your hand along the wire luff to make sure the sail isn't twisted. Attach the hanks to the forestay by pushing and twisting.

4 Check you have the right halyard, and it isn't twisted.

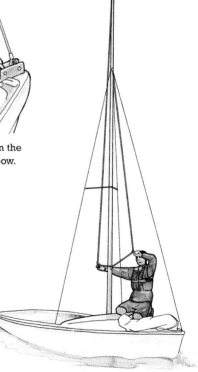

5 Attach the halyard (halyards pull up sails).

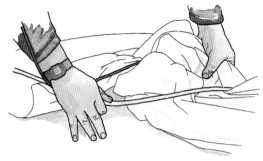

6 Leave the jib down, secured by the painter.

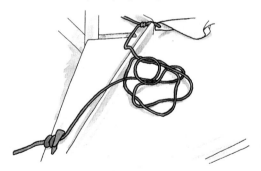

7 Rig the jibsheets through the fairleads, with a figure of eight knot in each end.

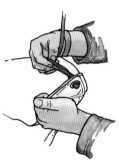

8 Unroll the mainsail, run your hand down the luff rope and attach the main halyard.

9 Pull up the mainsail (the crew feeds while the helmsperson pulls).

10 Cleat the halyard like this. Once round the cleat ...

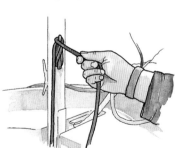

11 ... criss cross ...

12 ... and a locking turn.

13 Pull down the boom and fit it to the gooseneck on the mast.

14 Coil the halyard. Twist the rope clockwise as you make the loops.

15 Take the standing part through the coils ...

16 ... like this.

17 Tie half hitches and hang on the cleat.

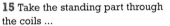

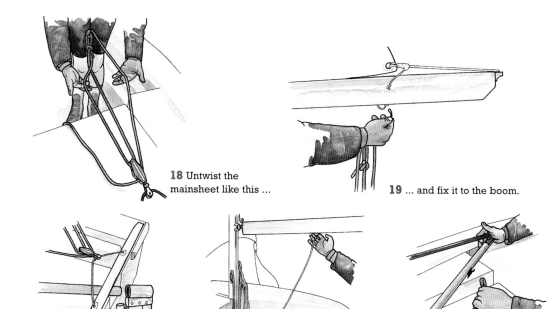

18 Untwist the mainsheet like this ...

19 ... and fix it to the boom.

20 Push in the tiller and secure it with the pin.

21 Raise the jib, and fit the kicking strap (vang).

22 Finally, pull down the rudder.

Points of sailing

Everything in sailing is related to wind direction.

A boat can sail across the wind - on a beam reach.
She can sail *towards* the wind - close-hauled.
She cannot sail directly into the wind - No Go Zone.
She can sail away from the wind on a broad reach, training run or a dead run.

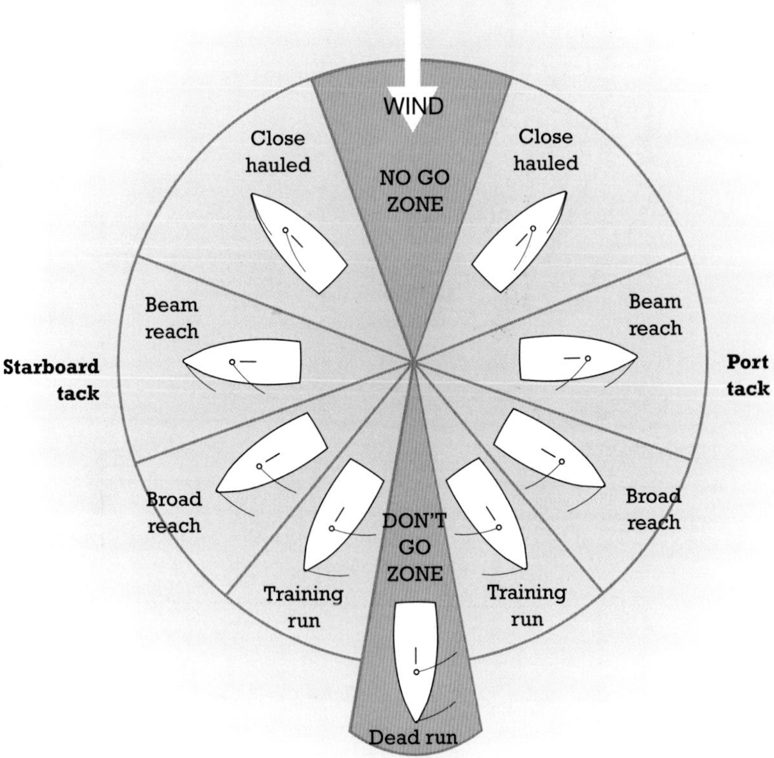

WIND

NO GO ZONE

Close hauled

Close hauled

Beam reach

Beam reach

Starboard tack

Port tack

Broad reach

Broad reach

DON'T GO ZONE

Training run

Training run

Dead run

WIND

NO GO ZONE

Close hauled. Sit forward. Centreboard down.

Beam reach. Sit in middle. Half centreboard.

Broad reach. Sit in middle. Centreboard three quarters up.

DON'T GO ZONE

Training run. Sit back. Touch of centreboard.

To turn round, tack

To turn round, gybe

Setting the sails

1 Choose your course, and hold it throughout.

2 Let out the sails until they start to flap.

3 Then pull them in until they just stop flapping. The sails are now set, until you change course.

A first sail

1 Begin in the lie-to position. The sails are out, the tiller is pushed away a little and the boat is hardly moving.

2 Check the wind direction. Feel it on your face, look at the direction of the ripples. See how the flapping jib blows away from the wind, like a flag. Seagulls usually sit facing the wind! In a moment you are going to sail across the wind direction, on a beam reach.

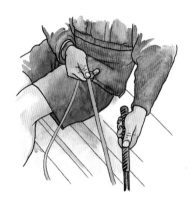

3 First, check you are holding the tiller in your back hand, in a frying pan grip.

The mainsheet is in your front hand. Sit on the windward side, well forward so the tiller clears your legs.

4 You pull in the mainsheet like this. Pull the sheet to the thumb, clamp it there, and repeat.

5 Let out the mainsheet by feeding it out; don't just dump it.

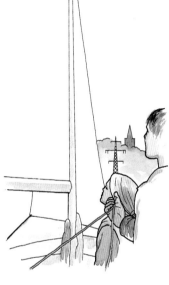

7 Watch to windward for gusts. In a gust you can either lean out or ease the sheet (or both) to prevent the boat heeling over.

6 Choose a PTS (Point to Steer) for a beam reach. Pull in the jib a bit. Steer for the PTS and pull in the mainsail until it just stops flapping. If you can see another object behind the PTS, great! Use it as a transit to keep a course.

8 If it all goes pear-shaped, hold the tiller and let go of the sheets. See which way the (flapping) sails point - this gives the wind direction. Usually, beginners end up head to wind. Pull the jibsheet on the helmsman's side to get going again.

How a boat sails

Make sure the centreboard is down.

Pull in the jib. The bow turns away from the wind.

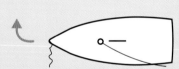

Let out the jib and pull in the mainsheet. The mainsail pushes the stern away from the wind.

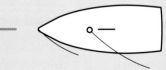

You can see how the sails must be balanced if the boat is to go straight ahead.

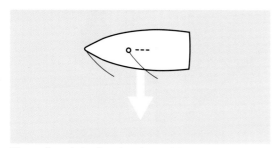

Now sail straight ahead and try raising the centreboard. The boat slides sideways.

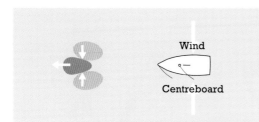

When the sails are trimmed and the centreboard is down, the effect is like squeezing an orange pip between your thumb and forefinger. The pip squirts forward, as does the boat.

Heaving to

We have already learned to lie-to. Now try heaving-to. With the boat stopped, back the jib and push down the tiller. The jib is trying to

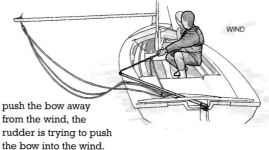

push the bow away from the wind, the rudder is trying to push the bow into the wind.

When the two are balanced you are hove-to, and stopped.

In a singlehander lie-to by letting out the sail. When the boat has stopped, push the tiller a little.

Tacking: stern mainsheet

The objective is to go from a beam reach going one way, to a beam reach in the opposite direction. If the bow of the boat turns through the No Go Zone, the manoeuvre is a tack.

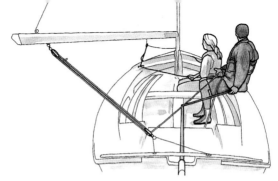

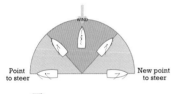

Point to steer

New point to steer

1 Sail at full speed on a beam reach. 2 Look to windward, ahead and astern to check the turning area is clear. 3 Choose a new PTS, ready for the new beam reach. (This will be directly astern.) 4 Say "Ready about!". 5 Crew checks centreboard is down, area is clear, and organises both jibsheets. They report "Ready!".

6 Think Hands, Feet, Sheet.
7 Hands: Put the mainsheet under your tiller thumb.

8 Pass the sheet over the tiller.

9 Separate your hands: you now have the tiller and sheet in the 'new' hands. 10 Say "Lee oh!".

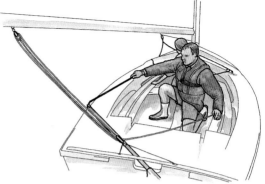

11 Feet: Put your front foot across the boat.

12 Sheet: Flick the sheet to make sure it's free.
13 Push the tiller hard, and keep it there until the turn is complete.

14 Cross the boat at the same speed as the boat turns, facing backwards. There's no hurry.

15 Sit down on the new site. Continue to turn until the new Point to Sail comes into view. Then straighten up.
16 Point the boat towards the PTS, and adjust the sheets.

Tacking: centre mainsheet

1 Prepare to tack as on the previous page. Put your back foot across the boat.

Point to steer

New point to steer

2 Push the tiller. Cross the boat at the same speed as the boat turns, facing forwards.

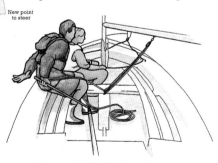

5 Bring your mainsheet hand to the tiller.

6 Let go with your 'old' tiller hand ...

3 Sit on the new side.

4 Straighten up. The tiller is behind your back.

7 ... and grab the sheet with it.

8 Finally, bring the tiller extension across your body and revert to the dagger grip.

Tacking: making it perfect

The crew's job

On the command "Lee oh!" let go of the old jibsheet.
Cross the boat in time with the turn. (You should
be in the middle of the boat when the boom is in
the middle.) When the mainsail fills, pull in the
'new' jibsheet.

Common mistakes of tacking

- Moving across the boat too early (**A**). You should be
  in the middle of the boat when the boom is central.

- Straightening up too soon (**B**).
  The boat is left in the
  No Go Zone (head to wind) and stops.
  Keep turning!

- Overtaking the tiller. Hold the tiller properly
  and at arm's length.

- Crew pulling in the jibsheet too soon (**C**).
  This forces the boat back onto the old tack.

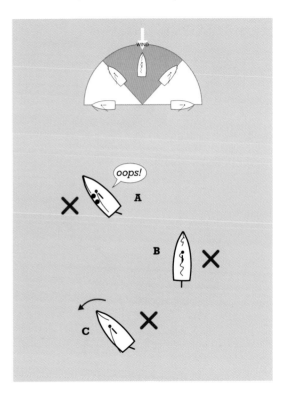

Getting out of irons

If you straighten up too soon the boat will stop, pointing into the wind. Push away the tiller. Pull in the jibsheet on the helmsperson's side. This backs the jib and pushes the bow round, so you can sail off.

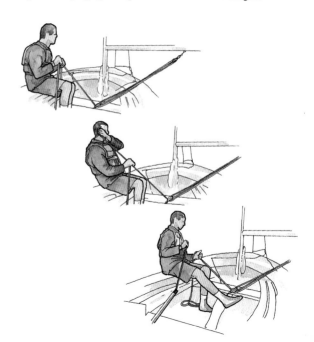

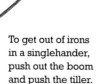

To get out of irons in a singlehander, push out the boom and push the tiller.

Pulling in a centre mainsheet

Use your tiller hand to hold the mainsheet while you change grip and pull in another arm's length.

The five essentials

The five essentials of good sailing are:
1 Sail setting.
2 Centreboard position.
3 Balance.
4 Trim.
5 Course made good (CMG).
Note: they are all linked.

Sail setting

As you turn towards the wind, the sails will flap
- so pull them in. When they are right in, and full,
you are close hauled. If they still flap you are entering
the No Go Zone - pull the tiller
towards you a little until the
sails fill again.

WIND

sails OUT till they flap   IN till they stop

sails in

sails out

On a beam reach, let out the sails
until they flap. Then pull them in
until they just stop flapping. Note
that pulling them in too far stops
the airflow over the sails: the boat
heels but slows down.

If you bear away from a beam
reach you need to let the sails
out, until the boom is just off
the shrouds.

Centreboard position

The more you pull in the sails, the more you will slide sideways. So put down the centreboard to counteract this. As you turn away from the wind and let out the sails, the forces point forwards. There is less sideways drift and you can pull up the centreboard to reduce resistance.

On a training run, all the forces are forwards. Just have a touch of centreboard in the water, to aid tracking.

If the boat heels, the sails are less efficient (because the wind blasts out of the top, not out of the leech). Also, the centreboard is less efficient (the water can slide under it). Plus the boat tends to turn up into the wind, because the water is bumping into an asymmetric bow shape. So keep the boat upright by leaning back, or by letting out the sails a little. If it's too windy, reef.

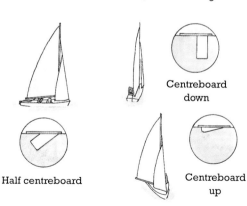

Half centreboard

Centreboard down

Centreboard up

To keep upright:
* Lean out.
* Sail out.
* Reef.

If you're heeling let the sail out a bit and/or lean out.

WIND

WATER

Trim (moving weight front-to-back)

Always sit close together, so the bow and stern can lift easily to the waves.

Helm and crew should be as far forward as possible up to Force 4. Above that move back a bit, especially on a reach and run.

With the weight in the middle, the bow and stern can rise and fall to the waves.

Too far aft. The bow can rise, but the stern can't.

Course made good

Be aware of the wind and tide (or current).

To go straight from A to B you will need to 'aim off', because the tide will take you sideways. If you can get a transit behind B, you can use it to 'crab' down the direct line.

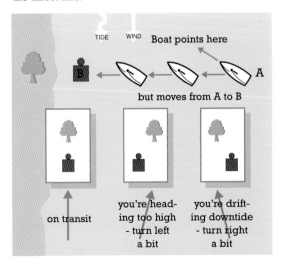

TIDE WIND Boat points here

but moves from A to B

on transit

you're heading too high - turn left a bit

you're drifting downtide - turn right a bit

Five essentials: summary

	Sail setting	Centreboard	Balance	Trim	Course sailed
Close hauled	In	In water	Flat	Front	WIND
Beam reach	Half out	Half	Flat	Middle	
Run	Out	Nearly out of water	Flat	Back (if windy)	

Turning from a beam reach to close hauled - luffing up

Put the centreboard down.

Simultaneously:

Pull in the jib gradually.
Pull in the mainsail gradually.
Turn towards the wind.
Lean back to balance the boat.
Keep turning until the front edge
of the jib begins to flap. You are
entering the No Go Zone.
Turn back a bit until the jib fills,
then straighten up.
You are close hauled.

Don't be satisfied - keep luffing
gently until the jib is about to
flap, then turn gently back to
close hauled.

When you are close hauled there
is no PTS - watch the front of the
jib and steer to the wind, which
keeps changing!

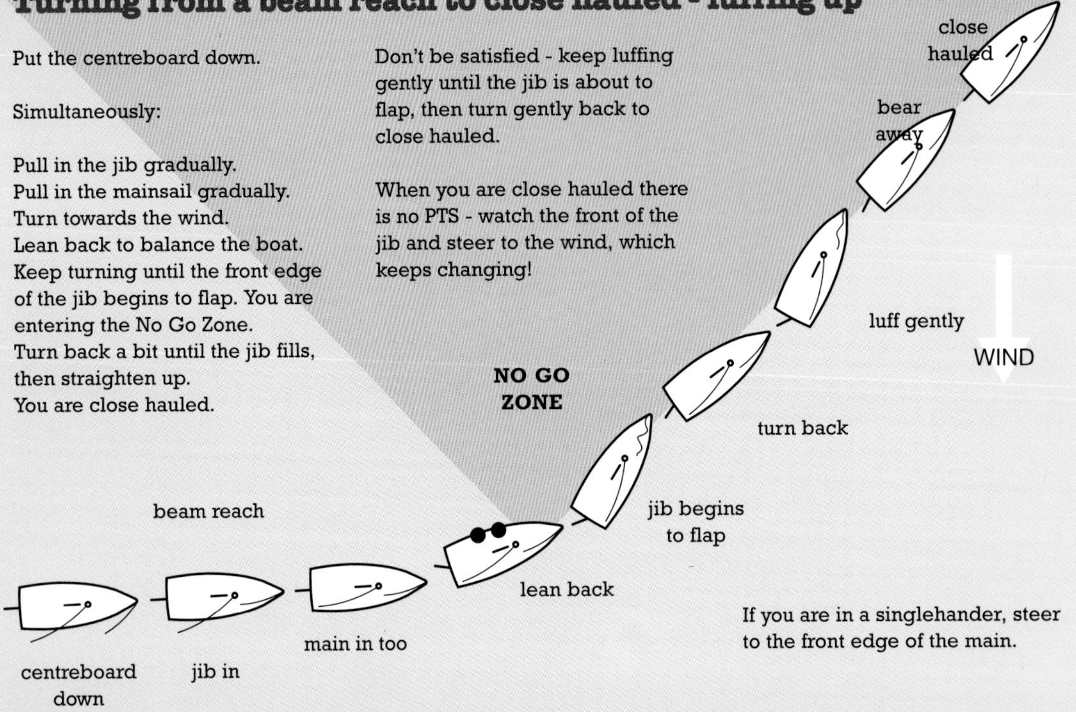

close
hauled

bear
away

luff gently

WIND

**NO GO
ZONE**

turn back

beam reach

jib begins
to flap

lean back

main in too

centreboard
down

jib in

If you are in a singlehander, steer
to the front edge of the main.

Turning from a beam reach to a training run - bearing away

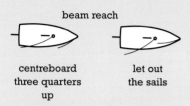

beam reach

centreboard three quarters up

let out the sails

bear away

WIND

sit in

Push up the centreboard until it is three quarters up.

Simultaneously:

Let out the sails gradually.
Bear away (turn slowly away from the wind).
Sit in: you will end up with one person on
each side for balance.
Watch the jib carefully. When it 'dies' (because
it is sheltered by the mainsail) you are entering
the Don't Go Zone. Turn back until it just fills,
and straighten up. You are now on a training run.

when the jib 'dies' ...

... turn until it fills

DON'T GO ZONE

training run

Beating to a destination upwind

Beating enables you to get upwind, from **C** to **D**. Beating is a series of close-hauled zigzags, joined by tacks. It is the only way to get into the wind.
Note that the No Go Zone 'goes with you', and you turn through it each time you tack.

If you want to get a rough PTS for the new tack turn aft and look over your back shoulder. That's approximately where you'll be going after the tack.

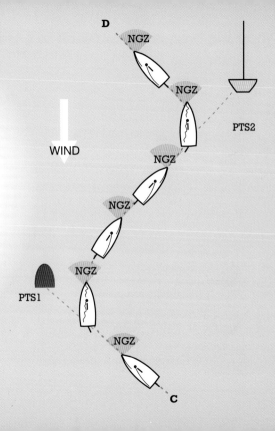

Advanced tacking

Keep the old jibsheet tight
until the mainsail has filled
on the new tack.

"Ready about!"

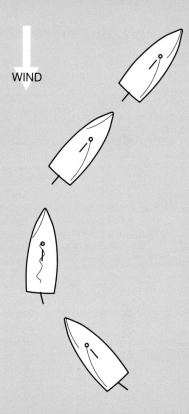

WIND

Gybing - changing course so the stern passes through the wind

You may need to go from one training run to the other, or turn to avoid an object. If you turn away from the wind, and the boom comes across, you have gybed.

Gybing with a stern mainsheet

- From a beam reach, let out the sails.
- Pull up the centreboard, leaving a little 'skeg' in the water.
- Move your weight in.
- Straighten up on a training run.
- Now look under the boom to check for obstacles.
- Say "Stand by to gybe!".
- Crew gets ready and says "Standing by!".
- Pull in one arm's length of sheet (so the boom will miss the shroud after the gybe).

- Think Hands, Feet, Sheet.
  Hands
  Change hands as for a tack.
  Feet
  Put your front foot across.
  Sheet
  Flick the sheet.

- Move to the middle of the boat, facing backwards.
- Say "Gybe oh!".
- Push the tiller towards the side you were sitting on.
- As the boom crosses the centreline, move across the boat and straighten up the tiller.
- Establish a new training run.

The crew changes from one jibsheet to the other as the boom comes over and moves as necessary to balance the boat.

1 Use the jib as an indicator to get on a training run.

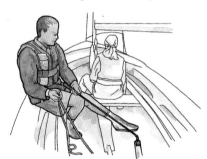

5 Put your front foot across.

2 Take mainsheet across the tiller.

3 Grip it under your thumb.

4 Separate your hands.

6 Turn.

7 Flick the sheet. Straighten up.

8 Sit on the new side.

Gybing with a centre mainsheet

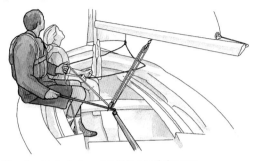

1 Use the jib to help establish a training run.

2 Put your back foot across. Then bear away.

5 Take the sheet to the tiller.

6 Let go with your front hand.

3 Pull the sheet. Straighten up as the boom goes over.

4 Move to balance the boat. The tiller is behind your back.

7 Grab the sheet with your front hand.

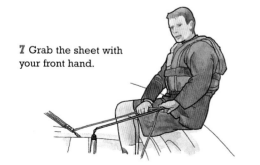

8 Separate your hands. Take the tiller across your body.

Reefing (reducing the mainsail)

If possible, tie up to a buoy. If not, heave-to in clear water. (Cleat or tie the jibsheet to windward. Keep the tiller to leeward.)

1 Heave to. Drop the mainsail.

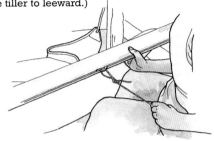

2 Replace the kicking strap with a reefing strop.

5 Put the boom onto the gooseneck.

6 Smooth out the rolls of sail, and pull them tight.

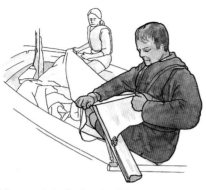

3 Take a tuck in the leech of the mainsail, to keep the boom up once set.

4 Roll the mainsail around the boom; make more turns if the wind is blowing hard.

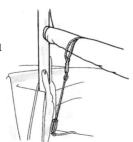

7 Hoist the mainsail. Attach the old kicking strap to the reefing strop, and tighten it.

8 Now the mainsail is more controllable.

Useful knots

Figure of eight. *Use:* a stopper knot.

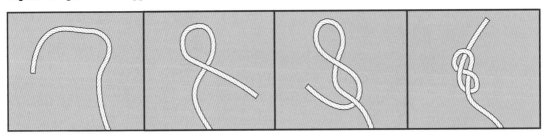

Round turn and two half hitches. *Use:* mooring.

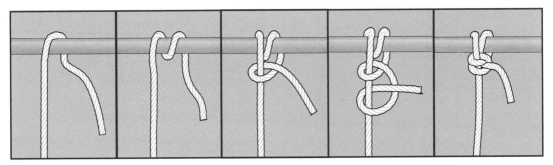

Clove hitch. *Use:* a quick release knot.

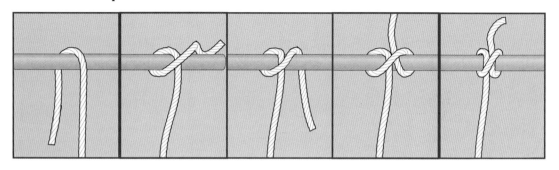

Sheet bend. *Use:* joining two ropes of unequal thickness.

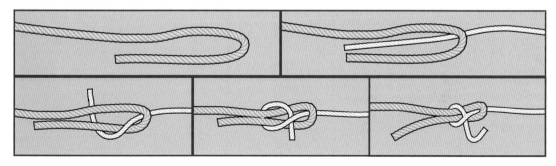

Bowline. *Use:* a loop that won't slip.

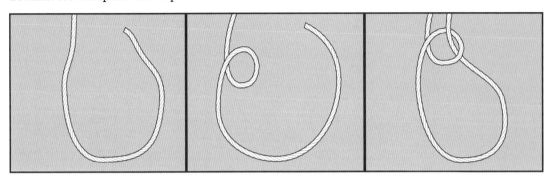

Reef knot. *Use:* joining two ropes of equal thickness. Releases easily.

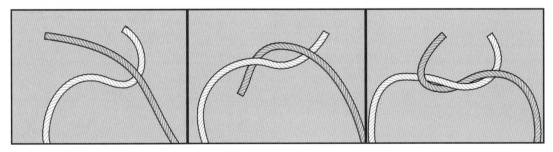

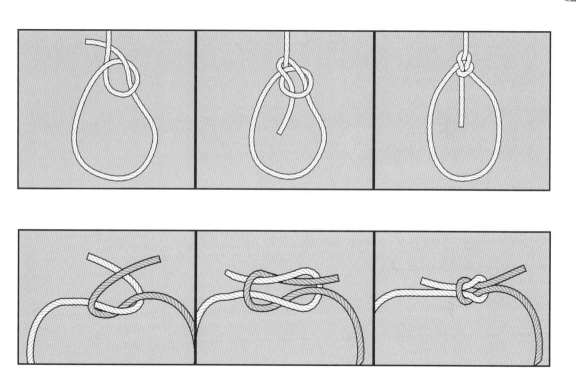

Rules of the road

1 **Avoid collisions at all costs!**
2 **For boats on opposite tacks:**
   Port gives way to starboard.

You are on starboard tack if your sail is on the port side. Usually the helmsman will be sitting on the starboard (right) side. "If you're on the right, you're in the right." Starboard tack has right of way over port tack (here **S** has right of way over **P**).

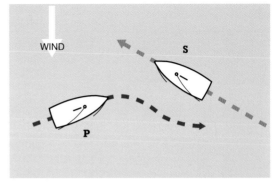

S has a duty to hold his course.
P has a duty to avoid the collision.

3 **For boats on the same tack:**
A Windward boat (W) must keep clear of a leeward boat (L).
W is, after all, taking L's wind!

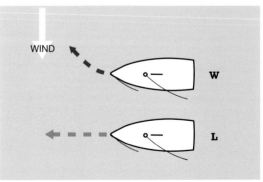

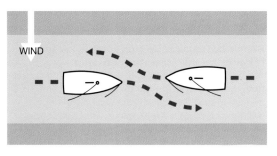

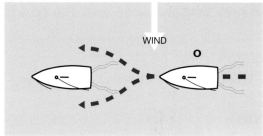

4 In a narrow channel turn right to avoid confusion (ie pass port to port).

5 A motorboat should give way to a sailboat, unless restricted by her draft (ie she will hit the bottom if she alters course).

6 The overtaking boat (O) keeps clear.
She can choose to go either side.

If a large boat makes one blast ◀–
she is turning to starboard.

Two blasts:	◀––	she is turning to port.
Three blasts:	◀–––	she is going astern.
Five blasts:	◀–––––	she is asking if you've seen her.

7 Some shapes and their meanings.

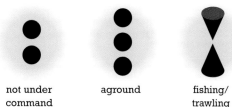

anchored   motor sailing   not under command   aground   fishing/ trawling

Assessing the area and the conditions

- The best source of hard knowledge is the locals.
- Look at a chart of your sailing area.
- Obtain tidal information.
- Take a bucket, paddle, first aid kit, and a whistle.
- Obtain weather information.

Tides

Roughly speaking, the tide comes in (floods) for six hours and goes out (ebbs) for six hours. The tide hardly runs in the first hour after high tide. Then it speeds up to a max at half tide, before decreasing towards low tide. The rule of twelfths is useful.

In the first hour 1/12 of the volume of water runs out (or in), in the second hour 2/12. Overall:

first	1/12
second	2/12
third	3/12
fourth	3/12
fifth	2/12
sixth	1/12

Every fortnight the high tides are very high and the low tides are very low - these are spring tides.

Every other fortnight the high tides are low and the low tides are high - these are neap tides.

Note that the depths on the chart (eg 3_2 meaning 3.2 metres) are for the 'lowest ever' tide. So there is usually a bit more water than this, and at high tide there could be a lot more.

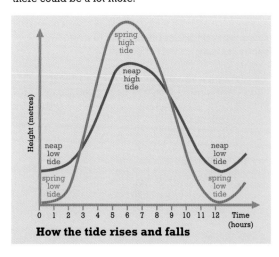

How the tide rises and falls

How to check which way the tide is going

- Look at the flow past a fixed buoy, post etc.
- Boats anchored at the bow lie to the tide.
- Tide tables.
- Let the sails flap and see which way the boat drifts.
- Large buoys lean over.

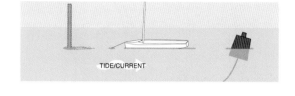

TIDE/CURRENT

Buoyage

Lateral (side) channel marks show you the channel.

They are colour coded for when you come into a harbour or channel, on the flood tide.

Don't tie up to navigation buoys, and give posts a bit of a berth because they are often set in the mud to the side of the channel.

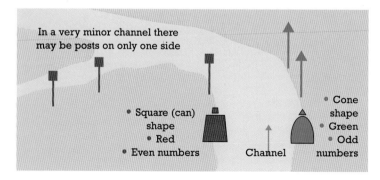

In a very minor channel there may be posts on only one side

- Square (can) shape
- Red
- Even numbers

Channel

- Cone shape
- Green
- Odd numbers

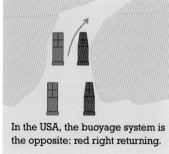

In the USA, the buoyage system is the opposite: red right returning.

How to call for help

- Let off a distress flare.

- Wave your arms like this.

- Hoist the jib
upside down.

- Make a continuous
sound - eg blow
a whistle.

Sailing a triangular course

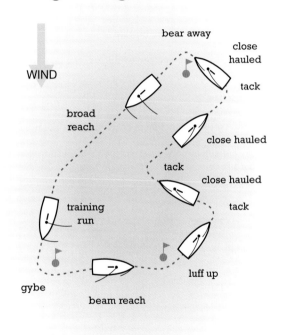

bear away

close
hauled

WIND

tack

broad
reach

close hauled

tack

close hauled

training
run

tack

luff up

gybe

beam reach

Capsize drill: singlehanders

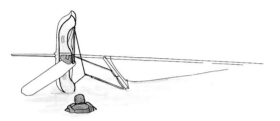

1 Keep hold of the mainsheet (your lifeline).

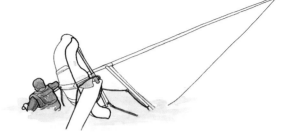

2 Swim round and clamber onto the centreboard.

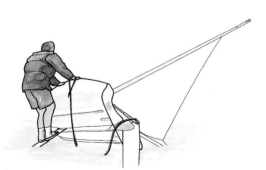

3 Grab the gunwale and lean back.

4 Scramble in.

Capsize drill: helm and crew

Capsize drill

 Meet at the stern and make sure no one is hurt. Also check the rudder is still on.

2 The helmsperson uses the mainsheet as a tether, to keep them connected to the boat, and swims around to the centreboard.

3 The crew swims between the boat and the boom, and pulls down the centreboard. Then they throw the top jibsheet over the boat to the helmsperson, being careful not to invert the boat. Finally they lie in the water, taking care not to pull down on the boat (which will hinder the righting process).

Problems

If the boat has capsized to windward and the mast is lying upwind, the boat may capsize again when she is pulled up. So the helmsperson first swims to the bow (holding the mainsheet as a tether) and swims the bow around to a rightable position.

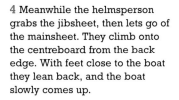

4 Meanwhile the helmsperson grabs the jibsheet, then lets go of the mainsheet. They climb onto the centreboard from the back edge. With feet close to the boat they lean back, and the boat slowly comes up.

5 The helmsperson is left hanging onto the gunwale (edge of deck). The crew is scooped into the boat.

6 The crew pulls the helmsperson aboard. Finally, they bail out.

Problems

If the helmsperson is too light to right the boat, the crew and helmsperson swap jobs. If both are light, then both can stand on the centreboard.

Picking up a buoy

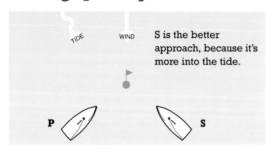

S is the better approach, because it's more into the tide.

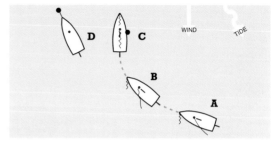

Tide is the critical factor when picking a buoy, because it's your brake.

Remember: 1. Plan   2. Approach
           3. Manoeuvre 4. Escape route

Tide with wind

Plan Usually one tack is better, because when you get head to wind the boat is pointing more directly into the tide (**S** rather than **P**). Tell the crew which side to grab the buoy.

Approach Approach on a close reach, aiming for a point one length downwind of the buoy.

Manoeuvre When you get a few lengths from the buoy let the jib flap (**A**). Use this as an indicator as to whether the main can be made to flap when you stop. When you reach the one length point, ease out the mainsail and luff (push the tiller) (**B**). The crew picks up the buoy by the windward shroud (**C**) and attaches the painter, using the fairlead.
As soon as the boat is connected, raise the centre-board and drop the sails (**D**).

Escape route

If the manoeuvre fails first time, bear away onto a beam reach and try again later.

Picking up a buoy – Wind against tide

Plan You must finish pointing into the tide. But if you approach in this direction you will be on a run and, with the main up, can't stop. Solution: take down the mainsail and approach under jib. Tell the crew which side to grab the buoy.

Approach Sail well to windward of the buoy on a close reach. Let the jib flap (**A**). Go head-to-wind and drop the mainsail (**B**). Back the jib (**C**), turn and aim for the buoy.

Manoeuvre Control the speed with the jibsheet - let it out to slow down (the jib will blow forward), pull it in to speed up (**D**). When you get to the buoy let the jibsheet fly (**E**). The crew grabs the buoy and attaches the painter, using the fairlead. Raise the centreboard, then drop the jib (**F**).

Escape route If the manoeuvre fails, round up into the lie-to position, hoist the main and try again.

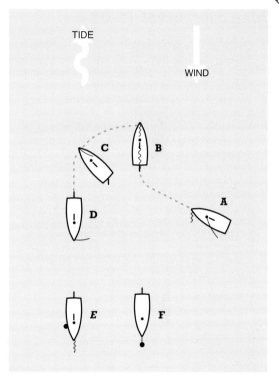

Man overboard! (MOB)

1 Check that the MOB is OK.
2 Although he will drift with the tide, make a mental note of his position: "He's between the two red buoys and opposite the tree".
3 Tell the MOB you will come back for him! Turn onto a beam reach (**A**).
4 Let the jib flap (**B**) - it is now your indicator.
5 Sail on this beam reach for 100 metres, to give yourself room to manoeuvre.
6 Make sure you have some speed, and the centre-board is down. Tack (**C**).
7 Aim towards the MOB. You are now going to check that you can stop when you get to him. Let out the mainsail (**D**). Does the boat stop? If yes, carry on. If not, aim down onto a broad reach.
8 After 25 metres, aim for the MOB, and let out the main again (**E**).

9 Repeat (**F**) until you can sail towards the MOB and stop.
10 Now sail towards the MOB, controlling your speed by pulling in and letting out the mainsheet (**G**).
11 Stop in the lie-to position with the MOB at the windward shroud (**H**).
12 Try to help him on board. If this is impossible, tie a bowline in the windward jibsheet and lower it over the side for him to put his foot in. (This also pulls the jib to windward. Push the tiller down, and you're automatically in the hove-to position.) Now you should be able to get the person aboard.

Note: A beam reach is good because you leave the MOB directly astern. He should be directly ahead after your tack onto a beam reach.

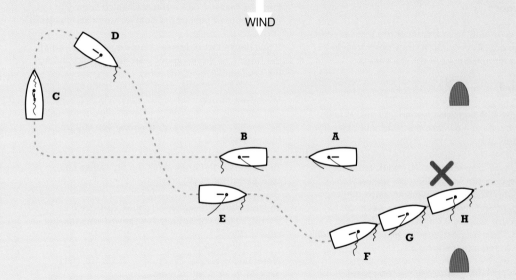

WIND

Launching and Landing

Cross shore

Launching or landing in a cross-shore wind is easy - simply go out (**A**) or back (**B**) on a beam reach. You can control the speed with the sheets.

Lee shore

In a dinghy with an onshore wind you are, at least, safe - if you make a mistake the wind will blow you ashore!

To land lie-to, drop the main (**C**), then head for the beach on a run, controlling the speed with the jibsheet. Before it gets shallow, raise the centreboard and rudder. In shallow water the helmsperson jumps out one side and the crew the other. Then they can run the boat up the beach, or turn it round into the waves.

To launch (**D**), the crew holds the boat head to wind by the shroud. The helmsperson climbs aboard and rigs.

Find the biassed tack – the one which takes you out best. The crew pushes the boat forwards and jumps in.

If this doesn't work consider rowing or paddling off the beach, or throwing out your anchor and pulling the boat out.

Weather shore

Be careful - if anything goes wrong you will be blown out to sea.

To launch rig the boat, back the jib and sail off on a broad reach (**E**).

To land beat in towards the shore. Approach on a close reach, controlling your speed with the sheets (**F**).

Note: that in almost every case you finish/start with the boat head-to-wind.

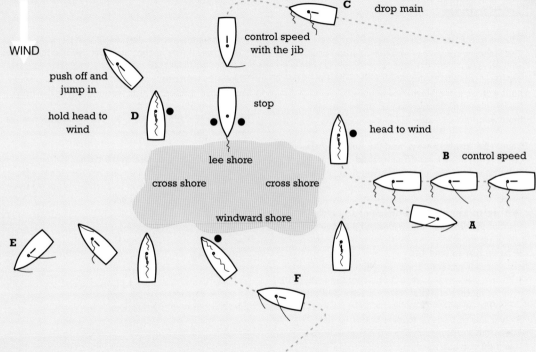

WIND

drop main

C

control speed with the jib

push off and jump in

stop

hold head to wind

D

head to wind

B control speed

lee shore

cross shore   cross shore

windward shore

A

E

F

Anchoring

There are four main types of anchor
The Fisherman's anchor and the Grapnel hold
well on rocks.
The Danforth and CQR (sometimes called the Plough)
hold well on soft material (mud, sand).
All of them work by digging in, as well as by
their weight.

Stow the anchor so it, and the line or chain, won't
come adrift if the boat turns upside-down. A good
solution is to screw a bucket to the floor, stow the
gear in it, and have a mesh lid on top.

Where to anchor Look on the chart for the anchor
symbol. A muddy bottom is best, in 2-3 metres of water.

Where not to anchor
* In a major channel.
* Near a marker post (you'll obstruct the view of it) .
* In the middle of moorings (you may collide when
  the tide turns).
* Over oyster beds or mussel beds.
* Beneath a pylon or bridge (the tide may rise
  and lift you into it).
* Above undersea cables (look on each shore for

a post with a yellow diamond).
* In seaweed (the anchor can't get down to the bottom).

When to anchor
Preferably, anchor at high water. Then as the tide
goes down, it extends the line.
If you anchor at low water, the rising tide may make
the boat pull out the anchor.

How to anchor: wind with tide
Sort out the anchor and its chain/rope. Make sure
the end of the rope is tied to a strong point eg the
mast or the centreboard case.

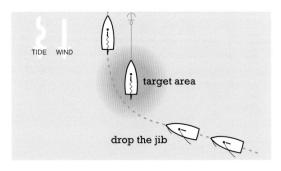

TIDE WIND

target area

drop the jib

Approach the target area on a close reach, and drop the jib (to keep it clear of the action). Sail well upwind of the target, turn head-to-wind and lower the anchor over the bow, running the rope through the fairlead. Allow the boat to drift back, still head-to-wind, until you're over the target.

Take a transit between two objects, and watch for a while to see if the anchor is dragging. Once you're secure, drop the mainsail.

Retrieving the anchor: wind with tide
Pull up the mainsail first.
When you're ready, hoist the jib, raise the anchor, back the jib and sail off.

How to anchor: wind against tide
Approach to windward of the target. Round up head-to-wind and drop the main.
Turn downwind and run past the target, controlling your speed by flapping the jib.
When you're well up-tide, flap the jib and drop the anchor. The tide will push you back to the target. Take a transit and, when you're happy, drop the jib.

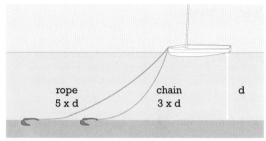

rope
5 x d

chain
3 x d

d

Retrieving the anchor: wind against tide
Hoist the jib and when you're ready retrieve the anchor and sail off. Then lie-to and hoist the main.

How much rope/chain?
If your warp is rope the length should be at least 5 x the maximum depth of water.
If you are using chain you must have at least 3 x the depth.
If you have rope with a length of chain connecting to the anchor, 4 x the depth is appropriate.

Kedging off
This is the only time you can justify throwing out the anchor. The idea is to get the anchor offshore, then pull the boat towards it. Repeat until you can sail away.

Being towed

Ideally, *you* want to be in control. Tie the towrope to your mast, then take it through the fairlead to the towboat and back through the fairlead to the mast. Wrap it twice round the mast and hold it - then if something goes wrong you can let go!

Take down your sails in case the towboat turns downwind. Pull up the centreboard or the boat will 'waterski' from side to side.

Move back as far as you can, with one person each side.

Leave the rudder on, and steer towards the towing point.

But if you're in a chain of boats being towed, take off your rudder or the boat behind may smash into it.

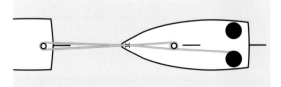

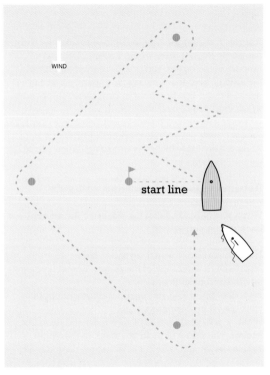

WIND

start line

Racing

A race is started from an (imaginary) startline, usually between the mast of a committee boat and a buoy. Your aim is to be just behind that line at the starting gun, travelling at full speed!

How do you know when the start will be? At 10 minutes to go a gun is fired and your class flag is raised (the warning signal). Start your stopwatch.

At five minutes to go another gun is fired and flag P is raised (the preparatory signal). Check your watch, or re-start it if your timing is out.

In the last couple of minutes, lie-to like A. Judge your speed and position to bring you up to the line just after the starting gun.

Now sail close-hauled, tacking as necessary, to the windward mark W, bear away and broad reach to the gybe mark G and broad reach to the leeward mark L. Then beat to the finish.

Right of way

While you're racing remember POW!
Port keeps clear of starboard (for boats on opposite tacks).
Overtaking boat keeps clear.
Windward boat keeps clear (for boats on the same tack).

Types of racing

You may be in a race where all the boats are the same (fleet racing). First across the line wins.

Alternatively, you may sail in a handicap race. Here the boats all start together, the finishing times are taken and the handicap applied to see who has won.

Racing is a great way to test your skills; we hope you enjoy it as much as we do. See you out there!

GLOSSARY

The boat:

Aft	-	Towards the stern
Amidships	-	Middle part of the boat
Bow	-	Front end
Fore	-	In front
Port	-	Left side if looking towards the front
Quarter	-	Back 'corner'
Starboard	-	Right side if looking towards the front
Stern	-	Back end

Position relative to the boat:

Abeam	-	To the side
Aft	-	Towards the stern (behind)
Ahead	-	In front of, in the direction of the bows

Astern	-	Behind, in the direction of the stern.
Downwind	-	On the side away from the wind
Forward	-	In front
Leeward	-	Downwind (opposite to weather)
Weather	-	Side of vessel nearest to the wind
Windward	-	On the side onto which the wind is blowing

Boat manoeuvres etc:

Aground	-	When centreboard rests on bottom. Back the jib (pull in the windward jibsheet)
Bear away	-	To turn away from the wind

Bend on	-	To fasten - rope to rope, sail to halyard, sail to spar
Broad reach	-	Wind over quarter (back corner)
Broach	-	Slew round when running so wind is brought abeam (ie lose control!)
Close hauled	-	As close to the wind as sails will work efficiently
Going about	-	Changing direction when bow passes through the wind
Gybing	-	Changing direction when stern passes through the wind
In Irons	-	Head to wind, unable to turn in either direction
Luff up	-	To bring front of boat closer or into the wind
Make fast	-	To secure a rope
Mooring	-	Making a vessel fast to a quay, buoy or posts
Pinching	-	Boat pointing too close to the wind
Reaching	-	Wind at right angles to boat
Reef	-	To reduce area of sail
Running	-	Wind coming from behind
Sailing by the lee	-	With the wind coming over the same side as mainsail.
Sternway	-	Backward movement of a vessel
Tacking	-	Zig-Zag course: to sail in direction from which wind is coming
Weighing anchor	-	Raising anchor from the bottom (sea bed)

Lifeboats
Offshore

We are pleased to donate advertising space within our books to RNLI Offshore. Registered Charity number 209603.

"As sailors, we can always count on volunteer lifeboat crews. Can they count on you? Please join *Offshore* today."

Sir Robin Knox-Johnston CBE, RD

However experienced you are at sea, you never know when you'll need the help of a lifeboat crew. But to keep saving lives, the Royal National Lifeboat Institution's volunteer crews need **your** help.

That is why you should join **Offshore**. For just £3.50 per month, you can help save thousands of lives, receive practical information to help keep **you** safe at sea **and** save money on equipment for your boat.

Call free
0800 543 210
Because life's not all plain sailing

Please join *Offshore* – today